MW01289561

To Asta,
Many blessings
in all you do!
Wendy Wells
Charampa

THE *UNSEEN* GIFTS OF ALZHEIMER'S DISEASE AND DEMENTIA

The Greatest of These is Love

WENDY CHANAMPA

BALBOA
PRESS

A DIVISION OF HAY HOUSE

Copyright © 2016 Wendy Chanampa.

All rights reserved. No part of this book may be used or reproduced by any means, graphic, electronic, or mechanical, including photocopying, recording, taping or by any information storage retrieval system without the written permission of the author except in the case of brief quotations embodied in critical articles and reviews.

This book offers the author's personal experiences and opinions about dementia. The author is not licensed as a physician, psychologist, or psychiatrist. While all the stories in this book are based on actual experiences, all names and identifying details have been changed to protect the privacy of the people involved. Some details in the stories have been altered for literary purposes. No part of this publication shall be reproduced, transmitted or resold in whole or in part in any form, without the prior written consent of the author.

Balboa Press books may be ordered through booksellers or by contacting:

Balboa Press
A Division of Hay House
1663 Liberty Drive
Bloomington, IN 47403
www.balboapress.com
1 (877) 407-4847

Because of the dynamic nature of the Internet, any web addresses or links contained in this book may have changed since publication and may no longer be valid. The views expressed in this work are solely those of the author and do not necessarily reflect the views of the publisher, and the publisher hereby disclaims any responsibility for them.

The author of this book does not dispense medical advice or prescribe the use of any technique as a form of treatment for physical, emotional, or medical problems without the advice of a physician, either directly or indirectly. The intent of the author is only to offer information of a general nature to help you in your quest for emotional and spiritual well-being. In the event you use any of the information in this book for yourself, which is your constitutional right, the author and the publisher assume no responsibility for your actions.

Any people depicted in stock imagery provided by Thinkstock are models, and such images are being used for illustrative purposes only.
Certain stock imagery © Thinkstock.

Print information available on the last page.

ISBN: 978-1-5043-5068-6 (sc)
ISBN: 978-1-5043-5069-3 (e)

Library of Congress Control Number: 2016902565

Balboa Press rev. date: 05/09/2016

This book is dedicated to everyone
living with dementia.

May your journey be blessed with rainbows in
the storm.

*Thank you to the following individuals who
without their contributions and support this
book would not have been written:*

My dad, Walter Wolfinger
*Sara Gray: for editing, abundant
consultations and reassurance*
Jill Burzynski: for advice, guidance and encouragement
Dr. William Beckwith: for advice and wise suggestions
Elizabeth Smith: for guidance, wisdom and prayer
*Debbie Miller: for continuously believing in
me and teaching me to be my best self*
*Luis Chanampa: for standing beside
me while I follow my heart*

To Love a person is to learn the song that is in their heart and to sing it to them when they have forgotten.

- Arne Garborg

CONTENTS

PREFACE

For me, working with people with dementia and their families is not a job. Rather it is a privilege – a calling. Everyday, my heart feels the love from someone with dementia or his or her family. Working as an advocate, I have had to seek out ways to communicate and interact with people living with dementia. Being legally and morally responsible for my clients, I am the one consistently making sure that their needs are being addressed. It is my responsibility to teach caregivers and families how to help my clients live well. To accomplish this, I have had to discover my own survival techniques and best practices.

The message that I deliver is one of love and acceptance of the person living with dementia. Learning to lay down our own agenda and live in their world is not easy, but once understood and experienced, positive life changes can take place. An emphasis on gentle self-love for the families is taught. Often stress and family disagreements overshadow the entire well being of the individual with dementia and a hamster-wheel scenario develops. The caregiver is exhausted and frustrated; the person with dementia becomes more difficult to interact with as their disease progresses; caregivers and family become increasingly stressed; the person with dementia may display agitation and become disruptive. This vicious cycle ultimately intensifies the difficulties for both the caregiver and the care receiver. For all to live well, this cycle needs to stop. To stop the cycle, I learned that I, personally, had to change. The person with dementia cannot.

This book is about teaching caregivers and families how to look upward to see the rainbow in the midst of the storm. Changing your approach changes everything and you will learn, step by step, how to see past the dark clouds with love and gratitude. Exploring your own fears, learning to live in the moment, and letting go of your expectations creates a pathway of survival through the Alzheimer's disease and dementia continuum.

I am grateful for the experiences and the opportunities that I have acquired through my career as a professional guardian, private care manager and dementia care trainer. I have learned so many things from my clients. I often teach others how to interact with compassion and love, despite the circumstances. Practicing living in the present with people with dementia has been the most fulfilling part of my professional life and can make an incredible difference in the lives of those living with this disease and their caregivers. Dementia is not going away, and the time has come for the focus to be on living well with this disability. Advocating for excellent care and training caregivers and family members, while expressing love in the moment, has been an ever-evolving path. It is time now to share the lessons that I have learned through my personal and professional baptism by fire!

This book focuses on teaching others how to see the hidden gifts that are everywhere in this relentless journey through dementia and Alzheimer's disease. There are so many opportunities to see the rainbows in the midst of the storm, if we can learn to stop, look up and recognize that the person living with dementia is still there, just different. As we learn a new dance and a new song, we and our loved ones with dementia can truly thrive.

CHAPTER 1

The Gift

"You gain strength, courage, and confidence by every experience in which you really stop to look fear in the face. You must do the things which you think you cannot do".

— Eleanor Roosevelt

Walter began to repeat himself. He began to have difficulty getting up from his chair. For years he had a sort of shuffle to his walk and blamed it on his "bum knee." His wife noticed that he was often short and angry with her. He began accusing her of an extramarital affair. After months of gradual changes in his personality and moods, and increasing difficulty with his mobility, his daughter, a nurse, encouraged him to see a neurologist. Walter, or Wally, as he preferred to be called, was 82 years old. He reluctantly agreed to a neurological assessment and evaluation. After hours of testing, the day arrived for the results to be shared. Wally was confident that he was fine and was convinced his knee was the problem. His wife was uncertain, thinking maybe she was exaggerating things in her mind. She told the family, "He is not really that bad, just occasionally he seems different."

"Walter, you have Parkinson's Disease and dementia," the doctor, without emotion, told Wally and his wife. That was it. No suggestions of assistance, no direction and certainly no explanation. "Walter, You have Parkinson's Disease and dementia." Neither Wally nor his wife accepted this diagnosis and lived in denial for the next two years. As his mobility decreased, Wally decided that he was going to have his "bum knee" fixed. His family argued against it. Several surgeons told him that he should not risk the surgery, but finally he found a surgeon willing to operate. The actual operation went well, but after an infection set in, a second emergency surgery kept him under anesthesia for more than four hours, which exacerbated his dementia and changed the progression of his disease. Life would never be the same.

After discharge from the hospital, Wally spent a few months in a rehabilitation center hoping to regain some of his mobility and orientation. Unsuccessful at best, Wally was sent home with a wheel chair, minimal assistance and little hope. He purchased an electric wheel chair that he was never able to learn to operate safely (proven by the dents on the wall). His family was left to deal with his disorientation, immobility and moderate aggressiveness.

All of Wally's symptoms continued to worsen and he became more confused daily. There was little that could be done to help him. He would try to get up and walk, forgetting that he was unable. EMS or a kind neighbor would be called to lift him off the floor. He refused his medicine because he thought that he did not need it. After several months of just getting by, his wife became unable to keep up with the daily demands of caring for someone with dementia. Her health began to fail due to exhaustion. Fortunately, Wally had children who were willing to help. Although they did not live locally, they began to offer assistance, but the primary responsibility still remained on his wife's shoulders.

Wally was placed on Hospice care and a part time aide was hired to assist with his care at home. His daughters took turns visiting and offering emotional and physical support.

Having to change your parent's incontinence brief can be a very difficult and gentle act of love. The family spent the next several months celebrating Wally's life, while he was alive and able to participate. Through difficult days and nights, they sought to find the humor and strength that Wally needed. They held each other's hands and lifted each other's spirits. Wally could sense this calmness and spirit of love. There were days that he was extremely difficult, insisting that his wife was sneaking out with another man, and sometimes he refused to take a shower. He would forget that he had just eaten and would tell others that he was not being fed. Often he walked into the days of his youth, seeing and describing friends that had passed on, as if they were standing outside his window. Attempts to take him out for walks and fresh air were fought with excuses. It was obvious, Wally simply felt safest in his own home.

I perceived that Wally knew that he was declining, but he could not admit it. Perhaps it was his survival skills kicking in or maybe complete lack of self awareness. Whatever the case, Wally told his family that he was fine and continued to blame that bum knee. He saw no need for help and fought personal care assistance daily. One day while his daughter was changing him, he became agitated and hit her across the chest. Surprised and devastated, she knew enough to not fight back.

"Dad," she said with tears in her eyes, "I am here to help you." Wally immediately stopped fighting her. It was not the words that were used that calmed him, but rather, the sincere, raw emotion that his daughter shared openly and candidly. It was not angry frustration that came across to Wally. It was pure love and compassion. As their eyes met, they froze in time. Love was put out on the table for Wally to push back or to receive. There were no expectations. Had he continued to fight, the love would have remained steadfast. Wally made the unconscious choice to receive. This single event opened the doors for a very real connection. Communication with people living with dementia goes far beyond the words that are spoken. Their ability to comprehend what is being said diminishes as the disease progresses, but this does not mean communication stops. There is a very special nonverbal process of communication that can flow easily, honestly and freely. Wally showed me how and taught me a lesson, so life changing, that I would refer back to it, many times, during the next several years. This lesson is golden. He taught me that communication with people with dementia is possible throughout all stages of the disease. Learning a new way to communicate without words may feel awkward at first, but as you begin to experience interactions on a deeper level and begin to enjoy your time together, it will all be worth the effort. Discovering how your body language, tones of voice and facial expressions speak loudly to those with dementia is the first step towards dispersing the clouds covering your rainbow. Therein lies the first gift.

Wally was my father and I was the naive daughter, trying to find a way to love this angry man and create a way to connect to the one person who had influenced my life so deeply. My dad, in this moment, connected with me in a way that I will never forget. Here it was! Honestly and sincerely I surrendered! I was able to completely discard my agenda and just be. The next several months were spent in his world, and our family was allowed to feel and grieve, even in his presence. My dad and I spent evenings reminiscing about happy days together, watching old home movies and thumbing through old photographs. There were wonderful memories that we were able to relive together. He had given us, his daughters, a wonderful childhood and a sincere appreciation for nature. He passed on a love of the mountains and the woodlands that remains strong in my heart.

The biggest lesson that he taught me was the value and honor in telling the truth. A good man, and a rebel of sorts, he told us his story of joining the Navy at 16 years of age, then returning to finish high school after serving. As we reminisced and reconnected, the opportunity even presented itself to discuss the difficult days, many years ago, when my parents divorced. Healing was ever present during this time. As I would leave to return to my home and family, Dad reverted back to the days when I was a teenager. "What time are you coming home Wendy-O? Be safe and remember Dad loves you." When I returned the following week, we would pick up right where we had left off. "What time did you get in, Wendy? I was worried about you." My Dad and I walked together in his world full of his reality. It was here that we spent our time together.

The healing, love and compassion were so strong; I could literally feel it as I entered his house. There was no fear, no condemnation and no unrealistic expectations. My sister and I spent wonderful days and nights just hanging out with my dad. We were able to connect deeply to him and to one another, embracing Dad's world. His wife, my beautiful stepmother, was also able to walk there. She had reluctantly begun attending a support group where she learned coping skills and strategies. As she sat and listened to the wisdom and fortitude shared by those who knew and understood her journey, she no longer felt isolated. She slowly began to regain her sense of self. From that group, she learned that she was not alone. The group shared tips and coping techniques along with genuine emotions. She developed life long friendships that helped to carry her through my dad's journey, enabling her to reconnect with him and rediscover her love for him.

It is never an easy journey, but there are daily blessings. I have personally experienced the walk of connection and love through this disease and I know it is a better, stronger road than trying to do it all yourself. In trying so hard "to do" we get caught up in our own selves, forgetting to live, love and enjoy. We fight so hard for our own agenda that we struggle and anguish. When my father needed help, it was undeniably, very stressful. I was working full time and traveling up to three hours to his home, once or twice weekly. Taking some of my work with me to complete on the road was very demanding and chaotic, but I managed.

When I finally discovered the power in just being there, in his reality, my life changed. The gifts that I received in spending that time with him are dear and precious to me, and I feel in my heart that it was, honestly and simply, pure love that overshadowed everything. Being totally me, following him, in a very basic sense, was a gift. Please know that I am not implying that it was a walk in the park. There were tears and exhaustion, but mainly there was joy. There was joy in celebrating Dad's wonderful life and in celebrating his past and his present. Joy that so easily could have slipped by me had I not received the gift. There was the rainbow - God's beautiful promise of love in the midst of the storm called dementia.

Dementia is DEVASTATING. I will not minimize that fact, but we can readjust our attitudes and perceptions. We are going to be living with this in our lives, and now is the time to improve how we deal with it. Dementia and Alzheimer's disease is not going away. Statistics show it will continue to affect more and more people every year. According to Alzheimer's Association, 2014 Alzheimer's Disease Facts and Figures, Alzheimer's & Dementia, Volume 10, Issue 2, one in nine people age 65 and older has Alzheimer's disease. About one-third of people age 85 and older (32 percent) have Alzhcimer's disease. By 2025, the number of people age 65 and older with Alzheimer's disease is estimated to reach 7.1 million— a 40 percent increase. By 2050, the number of people age 65 and older with Alzheimer's disease may nearly triple. These statistics are astounding! People are living longer and the population of those 85 and older is steadily rising. How are we going to manage? Until there is a cure, we need to try to embrace those living with all types of dementia and accept, cherish and enjoy the moments together whenever possible.

You can learn how to look for the everyday "gifts" of love that people with dementia and their caregivers can experience. Living in the moment can be an incredibly wonderful thing. If you can take the time to step into that moment with your loved one, much joy can be given and received. Trying to be the perfect caregiver and lamenting mistakes only removes you further from the love that is waiting to be experienced. You are not ever going to reach perfection in this life. Be gentle with yourself and know that just as people with dementia are doing the best that they can, so are you. You are an amazing person and a wonderful caregiver. You are human and have emotions and limits that have been tried and tested. Please stop beating yourself up. When mistakes happen, learn what you can, let it go and make amends as best you can. Forgive yourself, then move forward and step into the moment and see the gift.

As a Dementia Care Trainer, Professional Guardian, Care Manager and as a daughter, I have had the privilege and heartache of seeing this disease from multiple sides. Watching families slowly lose their loved ones has been heartbreaking. Seeing my father, the strong, nature loving, Pennsylvania Dutch man, slowly lose his abilities was terrible. But I choose to look for the blessings, for the rainbow, instead of magnifying the painful obvious facts.

Beyond the circumstances, there was a multitude of gifts waiting to be unwrapped. Most family and professional caregivers want to lovingly and proficiently care for people with dementia. In reality, this is extremely difficult. People with memory issues and dementia can present challenging behaviors. Caring for them is exhausting. As body functions, executive skills and memory deteriorate, caregiving often becomes overwhelming. Caregivers often neglect themselves as they work tirelessly to provide excellent care for their loved one. This behavior can be changed. Learn to step back, seek assistance and begin to unwrap the gifts. I promise you, they are there.

What transformed inside of me during this period with my father is also available to you. Each one of us has an incredible reservoir of intuition that can assist us with the unimagined world of dementia. By learning to let go, preparing ourselves to follow, and allowing the present to be, it is possible to glimpse - and even walk calmly and lovingly – into our loved one's world. This journey brings amazing joy. As we learn to follow this intuition, it can direct us and guide us with a new understanding of others and ourselves. Through this daunting journey, there are many refreshments and an endless well of blessings waiting to be discovered. People with dementia can live a good life. They simply live in a different reality. Once we stop insisting that they come back into our reality, hold their hand and permit them to thrive exactly where they are - new and beautiful experiences can happen.

Step by step, without pressure, we will explore the possible paths that are available for you. Together, we will let go of imagining how it was supposed to be. We will let go of others expectations about our performances as caregivers. We will learn to let go of what is not helpful and focus on self-honesty and simplicity. I did this by opening myself up to the daily events and allowing myself to be present without expectation or premeditation of the outcome. Daily, I had a choice to walk in fear or to walk, plain and simply, in God's love, moment by moment. Each time that I chose fear, the path was difficult and painful. When I chose love, there was something quite liberating and refreshing about it. In the midst of the storm, there was the rainbow. Thank you Dad for this beautiful gift and your lesson on being present for loving communication.

CHAPTER 2

What We Fear

"Courage is not the absence of fear, but rather the judgment that something else is more important than one's fear. The timid presume it is lack of fear that allows the brave to act when the timid do not. But to take action when one is not afraid is easy. To refrain when afraid is also easy. To take action regardless of fear is brave."

— Ambrose Hollingworth Redmoon,
from **No Peaceful Warriors!**

Every Thursday I would visit Elizabeth, who was early in her journey through dementia. She had several lawsuits pending and her mental competency was now being questioned. As her confusion increased, she began to incessantly blame others for her everyday shortcomings. She blamed the facility where she resided, other residents, her attorney and her daughter for her frequent falls, poor financial decisions and lack of personal hygiene. It was never Elizabeth's fault. She would say, "That man should not have been standing in front of me. If he was not there I could have grabbed the railing and I would not have fallen." She called her attorney and pursued yet another wrongful injury case. Everyone and everything was at fault, but never Elizabeth. There was nothing wrong with her. She was just fine and constantly told me that she was moving back to her home any day.

She knew that she was not going home and she had a very real awareness of her declining memory and reasoning abilities, yet insisted that she was fine and focused on blaming others to keep from facing her own fears. Elizabeth was unable to accept the fact that she had dementia and was not able to let go of her life as she knew it. It was clear that her subconscious decision to blame others was fear based. As she continued to decline, her accusations increased. It took some time, but eventually, Elizabeth and I grew very close. She trusted me and began to open up about those fears. As she acknowledged them, little by little, she was able to face her fears honestly. As she discussed her heartfelt fears courageously, space opened wide for gratefulness to flourish. I offered no judgments or solutions, just simply sincere validation of her feelings. Our visits touched me deeply and she will forever be a part of me. Beneath that river of fear and blame was a very strong, independent, brave woman.

As time went on, healing and courage began to rise up inside of Elizabeth. Acceptance and forgiveness emerged and Elizabeth lived out the rest of her life with joy and thanksgiving. Eventually, although her circumstances did not change, her life transformed. Visits with her family and friends, once again, became a pleasant experience. Her staff of caregivers was now able to get to know and enjoy the person Elizabeth truly was, beyond her fears. They no longer dreaded going into her room. She finally smiled and laughed again and was able to gracefully part from this world surrounded by her loved ones.

A large element of fear is often attached to facing any type of dementia, and denying fear creates a major roadblock in your journey. To the person with dementia, that first diagnosis carries a huge package of unknowns and what ifs. Just the mention of dementia or Alzheimer's disease conjures up visions of wasting away into oblivion, totally dependent on others to care for your daily needs. People feel embarrassed and ashamed of this diagnosis, fearful of what others think and not wanting to be a burden on their family. Often times, little hope is offered and one walks away from the initial diagnosis appointment with an overwhelming sense of emptiness and despair. All plans for the future are suddenly uprooted and self-initiated isolation is very common. Also, many people have been known to spend a great deal of time and energy trying to hide this disease from others or perhaps from themselves. One actually becomes extremely proficient with this process, especially during the early stages. It is amazing how well some can compensate for the short-term memory issues and lack of judgment that accompanies even the early stages of dementia. For most, they truly do not realize that they are forgetting and repeating themselves. Your attempts to make them aware may result in arguments and separation.

This is also the stage when one with dementia is particularly vulnerable to be taken advantage of emotionally and/or financially. Reasoning abilities are declining and the need to be accepted sometimes increases. Great measures may be taken to deny confusion without understanding what they may be signing or giving away. Often, the person with dementia has very limited understanding of what is going on with their assets. Social skills, long term memories and routines can remain through this period with appropriate answers and social niceness most of the time. During this phase, neighbors, friends, and some family members may have no idea that something is wrong. When things seem not quite right with a spouse, parent or friend, you may question your instincts. You may develop your own strategies for compensating and hiding any memory issues that the person with dementia displays.

You, the caregiver, may try very hard to keep everything together, while you, too, begin covering for the person with dementia. As you question and minimize the situation you may feel as though you are protecting and sparing them embarrassment. Many times, a spouse, covering for his or her loved one with dementia, suddenly has a health crisis of their own. You may relate to this overprotecting that sometimes takes place. At crisis time, you can find yourself totally unprepared and without support. Covering and overcompensating for your loved one's loss is a common method that you may use to avoid facing your fear as a caregiver. You try to act strong and hold on, but may be masking your own sense of devastation, projections and what ifs. To begin your healing and find hope, your fear needs to be acknowledged, recognized and accepted. This requires a deeper understanding of what fear is and what it is not.

Fear is full of projections and "what ifs". What if my wife does not recognize me? Is this treatment the best choice for her/him? Should we get another opinion? What if we can't do this? How can I watch her/ him go through this? What if I can't do this? Am I being selfish feeling this way? What if she/he dies? The list goes on and on. Fears are generally much larger in our minds than the actual situation and there are losses of energy in "what if" thinking.

For many of you, as caregivers or family members, the fear of losing your partner, parent or friend can be paralyzing. You are not alone. After initial diagnosis, as the disease progresses, many families express feeling their losses daily, as though they are watching their loved one die over and over again. The fear and pain compounded by the very real progression of the disease can leave you vulnerable to a downward spin, spiraling deep into your fears. You repeatedly relive your losses before your loved one is gone. Precious moments together are often lost or negated by the fear. Opportunities for joy, laughter and healing go by the wayside because of fear-based thinking.

Friends and relatives often are fearful about visiting: What do I say? How should I respond? What should we do? These are very good questions and sometimes keep people away. Their fears separate them from people living with dementia, long before they are gone, simply because of lack of knowledge and understanding.

Fear of the loss of control, fear of the unknown, fear of losing your loved one, slowly, to this disease, fear of death; it is all here. So how are you to move through it? How can you live with it? There is a not a one-size fits all answer. Fear is unique to each person; therefore a single solution does not exist. Acknowledging its very existence can be the first step to healing. Your healing opens you up to receive the gift of facing your fears and acknowledging the fears of your loved one living with dementia.

As if this disease is not difficult enough, now you have to face your own fears. There must be a better way! To explore your own fear takes courage and determination. You basically have two choices; to keep things just the way they are or to change. Facing your fears will bring change. Facing fears will not simply change your perception regarding dementia and caregiving. It will change your life and your approach to life, just as it did for Elizabeth.

There are steps that can assist you in this process. First, identify what you fear. Start with a prayer or meditation to quiet your mind, then breathe in and out focusing on every breath. Breathing is taught at child birthing classes and often suggested at small medical procedures. There is a reason for this. We are told, "Take a deep breath and let it out slowly." Exhaling is crucial and needs special attention. Concentrating on your breathing gives your mind the opportunity to focus on something else, redirecting your focus from the pain or anxiety.

Get quiet. Once you feel settled, create a mental list or write down your fears, one by one. Be completely honest with yourself. No one will be judging. This list is for only you. As you list each fear, feel the emotion attached; you may experience anger, grief, or disappointment. There are no right or wrong answers, just your answers! As you work through your list, feel the emotions that each fear has. Cry, laugh, scream or punch your pillow! There are no rules, except to feel the emotion within yourself. For some of you, this may be the first time you are feeling it, as life's circumstances and your belief system forced you to stuff these emotions. This is completely your time. Take as long as you need. Once you have identified your fears and felt the feelings, healing begins. You now get to choose what you will do with these fears and feelings. Are you willing to initiate personal changes? For some of you, intense feelings may have surfaced. Right now, as you recall these emotions, breathe in and out, focusing on your breathing again. You can do this!

Think back and recall any difficult times during your life. In the midst of the storm you could only hope that you would survive. There were no guarantees. But somehow you made it through. And if you look closely, you will see that you were not alone. There were support systems around you that cheered you on. There was your faith and there was your courage. There were rainbows in the storm! As you focus on your breathing, let things go. You are a survivor and you can do this. Seek out your support systems and professional help. If you have little or no support, recognize the importance of others to hold you up and cheer you on when you feel alone. Many others have walked this journey and survived, even thrived. They are there, ready to hold your hand, encourage you and assist you in this journey. Realize that being your best self possible is your greatest resource to assist you and your loved one with dementia. You can do this!

As you begin to release your fears, life changes. Yes, life changes! Begin your journey into the "now." This is where you are and these are your circumstances. You can choose to go with the flow or choose to resist. It is your choice right now. Resistance will keep you in a place of fear and strife. Let go, courageously, and know that there is a rainbow waiting for you to see it. Recognize the beauty. The universe always provides what you need at any given moment. You just have to discover within yourself how to find it. It is always here. By letting go of the fears you become open to see that your person with dementia is still here. He/she is a whole person, just different. You do make a difference as you embrace your loved one exactly where he/she is. Be present in the "now," letting go of what ifs and projections. Today, right where you are, enjoy your time with them. Unwrap hidden fears and be completely present. This is your gift from the universe; know that you are courageous!

CHAPTER 3

We Are The Solution

**"Sometimes the reason God doesn't show
up to win your battles is because he already
put inside of you the power to end it."**

— Shannon L. Alder

Joe was a quiet, gentle man. He had a very loving family that seemed to be able to accept him just as he was. Joe lived in his own home when I first met him, but as his dementia progressed, he had to move to an assisted living facility to ensure his safety. In the assisted setting, he adjusted well, but all of his professional caregivers, myself included, had to learn the steps to his "dance" to assist him while ensuring his independence and dignity. His daughter knew how to step back and allow Joe to do his own thing. She had already learned the steps to his "dance." The untrained caregivers lacked the skills and knowledge to be able to do the same. Several times a week, I was called to his apartment to prompt him to brush his teeth, take a shower and get ready for bed. The aides had no knowledge of how to encourage Joe to care for himself. Their method, very well intended, was to enter his apartment, smile and ask him if he wanted to take a shower. You will learn to never ask a question that you don't want answered. If the aides were able get the shower started, Joe would usually resist physically. This eventually led to him being labeled violent. In turn a request was made from the staff to the doctor for medication to prevent his agitation. It never occurred to anyone that it was not Joe having a problem; it was the staff's approach that was the problem.

Instinctively, not having a clue how to motivate Joe, I simply walked into his room, said "Time for your shower," lifted his arms and began pulling off his shirt. Joe looked into my eyes, smiled and surprisingly, he went with the flow. I handed him the soapy washcloth and motioned to him what to do. He responded and began to wash himself. It was as if all he needed was the start and the direction. He actually wanted to shower. It seemed too simple a solution, so I tried it repeatedly on several occasions and it worked again and again. I was able to demonstrate to the aides, my newly discovered solution. This solution worked most of the time, but when it failed I would try something else. It was that simple. Joe was not difficult to deal with, once I gave myself the permission to let go and act on my instincts. The answer came from inside of me. It was already there in the midst of the challenges. You, too, have the answers.

Caring for someone with dementia is always challenging. There is no single direct route, but with the right tools, you can become resourceful and learn the dance. Your responses to the seemingly inappropriate behavior will set the tone for the day. A person with Alzheimer's or related dementia cannot change but you can. You, my friend, can make a huge difference. Enter their world and open up yours. You can transform your life. Numerous books, classes and support services are available for family members and caregivers. Get the support you need. Professional caregivers are urged to read everything they can and attend every possible training class. New techniques are made available everyday. Behavioral interventions may work to adjust disruptive situations. Become informed and educated. Join a local support group and learn what has worked for others. Sometimes pharmaceutical interventions are needed for people with dementia and can improve quality of life. Learn to make informed decisions by researching and asking questions. You have unlimited resources of love, joy, happy times, and smiles that are still available for you and your loved one. By transforming your view of Alzheimer's disease and dementia, both your lives can change.

As you explore resources, you will see that there are many valuable tools and tips; but please note, you are human and cannot expect yourself to be perfect all of the time. Use the information as reminders and suggestions and pat yourself on the back with each successful interaction. You can be your own cheerleader. As you learn the steps and go with the flow, rainbows will appear. This is a promise. Little by little you can learn a new dance! This gift is forever in motion as we learn to twirl around the dance floor.

To learn a new dance, you must learn the steps. You probably do this by watching or listening first. Next you may take a few steps, feeling self conscious and uncertain. Perhaps you have a dance teacher or experienced partner. As you follow your partner's lead, you may feel awkward and silly. But you keep doing it and pretty soon…you've got the dance steps! You do not float across the floor like a "Dancing With the Stars" contestant, but you've got the flow beginning to surface. Now all you have to do is practice. Practice! Practice! Practice! Learning to be the solution is much like learning to dance. It will feel strange and at times difficult. As you partner up with a support group, an experienced caregiver or a wise, trusted friend, you can learn the steps. There are online resources for you to explore. There are wonderful support groups and there are many happy people living well with dementia. Of course they are not happy about having dementia. They are happy about living their life in this moment. You can learn to make a difference in your loved one's life and in your own life as well. Your perceptions about dementia can change and you can begin to breathe again. Breathe deep because there is still a life worth living. This is not the end, but is the beginning of a new phase, a new chapter. I know it is not what you had planned and it is certainly full of setbacks and challenges. Hang in there. Things will be different.

Let me tell you about Bob and Shirley. They impress me. They are a couple that I see occasionally at an assisted living community, while visiting my client. He is in great shape physically but his dementia is quite advanced. A handsome man with a fabulous smile, Bob can be full of energy. His attention span is very short so he is only able to sit for short periods of time. His wife Shirley appears to have learned to dance with Bob. He takes the lead and she follows. I've watched her as he curiously combs his environment. She relaxes. Bob lives in a secured community and the environment is safe and interesting. Shirley knows that this is best for Bob.

Talking with her, I discover that Bob is fairly new to this community, having moved in last year. When he lived at home, Shirley tells me that she could not keep up with him. She was exhausted and frustrated. He went from one thing to another, often becoming agitated and he needed constant supervision. When Bob's friends tried to assist, he became rude and obnoxious. Shirley had bought into the myth that staying home was the best thing for Bob. Very often this is not true.

Most people with dementia or Alzheimer's disease do not recognize that they are different. They are the same person, but appear different than they used to be to friends and family. Sometimes, the person with dementia can perceive a strange and unusual reception from peers. Early on, it may be the frustration from friends at the golf course when the person with dementia argues about no longer being able to keep score. Perhaps the repetitive stories annoy the bridge club members. Some friends just don't want to come around anymore because they don't know what to say or how to respond. Friends honestly don't know how to handle the changes and feel embarrassed and ashamed. Some are fearful of the very real possibility that they, personally, may be developing dementia. Whatever the reason for the distancing, the person living with dementia and their peers can sometimes experience uncomfortable feelings.

In an environment where most of the group has some sort of memory issue, there tends to be total acceptance. Fear and pretentiousness seem to disappear. Sometimes a secured assisted living community is the best choice. In Bob's case, it definitely was.

Shirley had made a wise choice. While she struggled for a year about the decision to move Bob to a memory care community she now sees, in retrospect, that the move was necessary to help Bob be his very best. He is no longer angry, restless or agitated and most importantly, he is safe. He is now in a place where it is ok to be Bob. Now Shirley is able to take care of herself and is able to be there for him. The staff is well trained to intervene when necessary and the community is structured to give Bob the freedom that he needs to explore and walk. As I watch Shirley, I see the love and dedication in her eyes. There is no longer pain and heartache as she watches Bob get up and walk across the room. I see total acceptance in Shirley's eyes. I see a woman who has had a very difficult road, finally living in the now. She smiles as he picks up the pillow and sets it on the table. Her smile is not counterfeit or forced. In total surrender to this moment, Shirley is experiencing the dance and enjoying it. You, too, can do this.

Whether your loved one is at home or in a facility there is a way to begin to enjoy today. Learn his dance and let him lead, gently guiding him towards those things where his success is guaranteed.

Caring for someone with dementia can have serious consequences on your health and wellbeing from the stress, sleepless nights and endless worrying. Please stop. It is up to you. Today, embrace the moment and step into the dance.

Let's look at how to begin. First, remember the breathing. Center yourself with a few deep breaths focusing only on that. As your body begins to calm, things should be a bit clearer. Now take a look at your circumstances. Things appear hopeless and often overwhelming. There is no other way to put this. Alzheimer's disease and dementia of any type will change your life forever. This is the raw truth. Acknowledge that truth and allow yourself to grieve. Grieve together, grieve alone, grieve in support groups, and grieve until you are ready to begin this new chapter. There is still a life worth living.

People living with dementia are still there. They are able to feel love and experience joy. They are whom they've always been deep inside. They change and become different in many ways, but inside, they are still there. This is a great contradiction: still the same person, yet different! They are still who they were before this devastating disease and in part, this compounds the tragedy. If a loved one was in a horrific car accident and had lost their legs, would this be any less tragic? Is it any easier to cope with a terminal cancer? Tragedy happens and is never easy. Again, acknowledge that this was not in the plans you had for your future. So now what? Do you forfeit your life, or do you choose to learn the dance? Can you choose to accept where you are and learn new things and a new way to be? If the answer is yes, you are on your way. Denial is one of the biggest roadblocks and can prevent you from ever stepping on the dance floor. If you want to learn to dance, you must get out of your seat, out of your comfort zone and move.

Once you have accepted your circumstances and acknowledged that dementia is now part of your life, you are up off the chair and ready to step on the dance floor. Now you will need a partner or instructor. Some of you may be surprised to learn that you can be your own instructor. I strongly believe that each of us has inside us the ability and instinct to just be. Those of you who had children often just knew what to do. Children did not come with a "how to do" manual. Perhaps you sought out the wisdom of elders and experts in the field. Ultimately, after seeking advice, you relied on your instincts to use the tips that resonated with you. Just as child rearing teachers and mentors aided you, so too, will support groups and experienced caregivers. They are willing and able to show you the steps. A vast resource of knowledge is available on line and there are dozens of books written on dementia. These are all very helpful, and what you need to rely on first and foremost is you. You can learn to go with the flow. Welcome wisdom and knowledge. Letting go of the fear and acknowledging your circumstances will open the doors to your heart. That, my friend, is where all your answers lie. As you learn to just be, the dance floor will no longer be intimidating. You will be able to relax and enjoy life again as you learn the steps. Today it may be a waltz, tomorrow the Twist! Life will not be the same as we learn to follow and embrace our loved ones steps. It will be different because this gift shows us that we are the solution.

CHAPTER 4

Unconditional Love: The Ultimate Love Story

"To Love without condition, to talk without intention,
to give without reason, to care without expectation;
THE SPIRIT OF TRUE LOVE." Author Unknown

Mary was beautiful. Undeniably well groomed with impeccable make up, clothing and hair. Paul, her husband of sixty-three years sat dotingly by her side. Mary and Paul celebrated their anniversary last month at the Memory care community where Mary resides. Paul tried unsuccessfully to keep Mary at home. Her daily wandering and agitation had taken its toll. Paul ended up hospitalized for a cardiac event and exhaustion. Their daughter, living out of state, had to force an intervention. Paul, now recovering spends his days grooming, feeding and dressing Mary at the memory care facility. Although the staff is able to assist Mary with all her daily activities, Paul insists on providing her care. Their daughter is comforted by the fact that her dad is able to get some sleep at night.

Paul presents another example of the heartfelt expressions of love that are ever present. Mary, if she were able to truly express herself, would insist that Paul take care of himself. Mary would tell us that she really is fine. She is content most of the time, loves the pet therapy dog that comes on Tuesdays and sings louder than anyone at the weekly sing along. Paul feels compelled to be by her side daily.

When Paul leaves at night, Mary sees the uncomfortable look on his face and knows that something is not right. She reacts negatively and expresses the fears and uneasiness that she senses. Paul sadly walks out the door with Mary sobbing in the background.

There is a similar demonstration of love every day in another memory unit. In this community, you see another woman, Agnes, hold tightly to the hand of the man next to her. The man barely notices his wife, Jane, when she arrives for her daily visit. He thinks that Agnes is his wife. The pain is evident on Jane's face as she pretends not to be upset. She tries to understand that it is the disease causing her husband of forty-two years to not recognize her. The staff tries to separate the surrogate lovers with no success. The gentleman becomes agitated and strikes out at the aide. His heartbroken wife, with a tear in her eye, tells the staff that she will leave. "Don't worry," she says. "I'll be back tomorrow."

You see this scenario played out over and over. Where is the gift? Where is the love? As people progress in their dementia they may no longer recognize children or spouses. The brain may fabricate and provide a substitute family. Yet the basic human needs remain, including the need to love and be loved.

How many times and how many spouses have experienced this? After sharing a life together, can you imagine watching the replacement of your affection with another? This must be undeniably sad and empty. It all seems so unfair.

It is unfair. Yet, love is there and so is the possibility of releasing the gift. The love is ever present in their hearts, forever, regardless of the disease. As the spouse, you have the opportunity to offer the ultimate gift of letting go. In holding on to what once was, you actually hinder the person with dementia from living their best life. Treasure your memories of yesterday. They are precious, but there may come a day when a choice must be made. Many spouses face this day of reckoning. To let go is the ultimate gift of love. Letting go does not mean that you agree with this cruel twist of fate. What it does mean is that you deliberately choose to accept it. You choose to accept your spouse, companion or parent exactly where he or she is. As painful as it will be, it is the ultimate love story.

Mary still loves Paul. Mary will always love Paul and Paul will always love Mary. They had sixty-three wonderful years together. Jane's husband deeply loves her, too, but no longer recognizes her. He will always love her. He has transferred his affections to Agnes because, in his reality, he believes that Agnes is Jane, his loving wife. The true, heartfelt love does not change. It is the expression of love that may change as the dementia progresses. The time together now will be different. In letting go, the spouses allow their loved ones the ability to live and love with dementia. It is not rejection. It is dementia. This gift is one that you can choose to give to your loved one. The cost is very high, but the gift of letting go is of tremendous value for both you and your loved one. They are still here, just different.

So much focus and attention is placed on what people are losing because of dementia. As difficult as it may seem, focusing on what is still there helps everyone. People with dementia have fun. They smile, laugh and argue with their peers. I was recently at a party at a dementia community. There was no one suffering there. People were dancing and singing. The two women that I sat with were cracking jokes and blurting out their thoughts. The lady to the left of our group was enjoying the magazine picture that she had neatly rolled up with a comb inside. She was very proud that she had figured out how to hide it under her jacket. She looked at me and asked if she could have it. When I nodded in approval, she was grinning from ear to ear. She was delighted.

There is so much joy, happiness and life amongst those with Alzheimer's and dementia; they are living with dementia! Their life is not over. They are whole and complete people, able to feel and give love with very real emotions. They are living in the moment, experiencing joy. Learning to step into that joy and dancing their dance will release your loved ones to live better lives. They can live well.

Holding on to how things used to be and clinging to the past will harm you both. People living with dementia may not understand why you are upset, but they do sense that something is wrong. You may think that you are hiding it. You are not. They can pick up on nonverbal cues, often with great accuracy. Their language and comprehension will fail long before their intuition and ability to sense emotions. You can reach them on that level whether you intend to or not.

Showing signs of distress, anxiety and chaos can have a huge affect on the person living with dementia. They can neither understand nor comprehend what is taking place with you, but they will usually react. They may react with anger, sadness, grief, anxiety and at times, aggression. Even in a crisis situation, try to remain as calm as possible. Toning down your voice and adding a bit of rhythm can help. For example, Joe is walking out the front door and he is refusing to come back inside. Speak softly, harness your panic and calmly try to guide him back inside. Walk beside him gently redirecting. Stay with him until you are sure he is safe. Try to follow his dance step, while gently guiding him to a safe path. What will work best is to lay down your agenda and follow his, while easing him in the right direction. You are still there and are a very present influence in your loved one's life. In letting go, you are not leaving them alone to do their own thing. You are simply allowing them to "be" wherever they are and accepting your loved one with unconditional love. This is the ultimate love story and the best gift that you can give is letting go.

CHAPTER 5

The Magnificent Mind

"If you change the way you look at things,
the things you look at change."

-Wayne Dyer

O ver the years I have learned that each person with dementia is different and unique, yet I had never encountered anyone like Patricia. She taught me so much. Patricia was an extremely intelligent woman and was very, very good at hiding her dementia. At our first meeting at her assisted living community, I quietly observed her as she appropriately interacted with others. Here, she seemed content and expressed absolutely no objections to her situation. All of her social skills were intact and she responded correctly to each question asked. She identified the date, where she was and all of her personal information accurately. Although she appeared not to have dementia, she also did not have any objection to her assisted living environment. Patricia's peers had obvious dementia and functioned at a much lower level than she. After a few hours I discovered Patricia's basis for survival; her magnificent mind. In her reality, the facility's community room was her place of employment and she had a fully functioning office, complete with clients, designs and staff. She moved stacks of papers in and out of the file cabinet, to her desk, then to the closet. The client files and designs had been purged a long time ago, but in Patricia's reality she was a very busy designer with daily work obligations, filing, and creating endless drawings. I entered her reality and became her personal assistant. This enabled me to hire and direct the professional caregiver staff and to organize her daily appointments. I became very fond of her and was amazed at her magnificent mind. I sincerely admire her ability to not only survive, but also thrive in her journey through dementia. It was incredible. Her own perception had somehow changed her circumstances to appear, at least to Patricia, that everything was on track. With little discontentment or disappointment Patricia enjoyed her days. To others her life may have appeared tragic. That was not Patricia's reality. She has lived well with Alzheimer's disease. There were difficult days where her reality conflicted with safety issues and scheduled events, but overall it was a good life. We had learned how to dance Patricia's dance. As time progressed, she trusted me to organize her daily affairs and most days she was content and living with a purpose. The aides were her assistants and she allowed them to participate in her daily routine. It was soon obvious that her dementia was quite advanced. She mixed things up frequently, but mainly, she made things up. Her fabricating was well developed and very believable. No reasoning or arguing would have ever convinced her that her stories were not true. You see, to Patricia, they were true, as this was her reality. Her magnificent mind had been able to compensate, through fabrication, to aid in coping with her symptoms of Alzheimer's disease, at least in Patricia's reality. When she could not remember, her brilliant mind filled the gaps with a "made up" story. Patricia believed that these stories were factual and acted accordingly. You can imagine the challenges that this presented, but Patricia lived well and it was worth the effort. Actively listening to her stories and not arguing or disputing truths aided our interactions. At times, she would become quite insistent about her perspective. Agreeing and learning to tactfully change the subject by introducing a topic that she loved would usually calm her. For example, if she insisted that she needed to go to the bank to withdraw her money, suggesting going later or tomorrow, yet not promising anything would often diffuse her, especially if another topic that she was fond of, was quickly introduced. She loved to talk about her days as a tennis player and that usually diverted her. Soon she was recanting old stories of her victories on the tennis courts. This happened often. Patricia's fabricating was her reality and we cannot change it, nor should we try. Gently leaning in a different direction, not ignoring her, but rather, listening, introducing a pleasant topic and moving on, tended to work most of the time. Her fabricating amazed me. In her reality, Patricia lived a very purposeful life. Her mind had compensated for the losses and made it all ok. Patricia had total acceptance of herself, as she was, enjoyed her reality and proudly walked in it.

What a magnificent mind we have. The ability to compensate for losses and the ability to survive are perhaps stronger than you or I could imagine. Patricia's reality counted for Patricia and for her loved ones. She had a good life and enjoyed it. She valued her work and felt valued by those around her. She had a wonderful family and continuous love and support. She lived well. Yes, her dementia continued to progress, but Patricia lived well.

Living well is a very broad concept and is very subjective. Feeling that you are part of a society and having your physical and emotional needs met is primary and a basic. In addition to that, for most of us, living with contentment and joy is proof of a good life. Assisted by her fabrication, Patricia lived a good life! She was loved and accepted exactly where she was. Patricia had excellent care and enjoyed her life daily. Many people that do not have dementia cannot make that claim. This gift is recognizing the wonderful ability of our brain to compensate for itself.

The marvelous mind, Patricia's mind, took the worries away by creating "stories" with happy endings. You and I possess that same capability. We can look at things from a new perspective and significantly change our reality. Applying the glass is half full or half empty scenario played out in Patricia's life.

Observing Patricia, the half full theory was quite beautifully demonstrated; in fact, in her mind, her glass was always full. I'm not suggesting that you, as a caregiver, begin to fabricate and make up stories, rather begin to allow your own magnificent mind to look at things differently. Open yourself up to the endless possibilities. If you see things from a slightly different angle, things will look different. Your perception sets up your story.

You can learn to see from a different perspective. If you look for the negative circumstances in your life that is exactly what you will see. The reverse also is true. If you look for the positive, magically, that too, is what you will see. Your own magnificent mind can assist you in your quest to see the positive things surrounding you. First, try to control your response to any situation. Know that even though you are not able to control your circumstances, you are able to control your response to it. Always, there are, and will be situations that occur that are capable of sending you into a tailspin. Stop and refuse to be sucked into the negative drama. You can change your response. Look for any positive aspect of the situation. For example, despite your circumstances, you have one dear and trusted friend you can always count on or you just met a person with a similar situation that has offered assistance. You now have respite care for a few hours a week. Perhaps you have good news from your children. The list goes on and on, but there is always some aspect of your life that is positive. Choose to focus on that, immediately. You get to choose how you will respond to any circumstance. Learn how your response can actually change the outcome as well as your feelings associated to it. When your mind interprets any event, it has a ripple effect regarding your personal well-being. This effect can be sending positive or negative ripples. How you respond determines which will occur. Remember, you and your well-being matter. Choose to use your magnificent mind to change your perception and you really can change your life. Recognize and honor this gift of your own magnificent mind.

CHAPTER 6

Learning To Live In The Moment

"Happiness, not in another place but this place...not for another hour, but this hour."

— Walt Whitman

Dottie is really special. She carries that spunk that lets you know that she will do what she wants to do and there is no persuading her otherwise. The first time that we met, the first words she said to me were, "I'm Italian. Push me and I'll shove you back!" Somehow I knew that I would love this woman. And sure enough, she stole my heart with her gorgeous black hair, big brown eyes and fiery personality. Dottie lives in the moment. Because of her feisty spirit, I quickly learned not to try to tell Dottie what to do. Things definitely needed to be Dottie's idea. So I had to allow things to be perceived by her as if I was just going along. I had to follow her lead and again, dance Dottie's dance. She needed to be in charge. During my visits, she would tell others that we grew up together and she would talk to me about her mother as if she were still living. Dottie was approximately 45 years older than me but that did not matter. In her reality, we were childhood friends, so I followed her lead. Reality orientation was not for this Italian lady. According to Dottie, I grew up in her neighborhood, visited her home and was one of her childhood playmates. That was just fine with me. I knew that to her, I was someone significant in her life and that I was a friend. Living for today worked for Dottie and her perception of the past interwoven with the present kept her living in the moment.

Each time that I visited with her, she was delighted to see me and we often reminisced about her childhood. She did not live in the past. Dottie clearly lived in the moment, not longing to go back. She shared her childhood with me as if I had been there with her. She rarely had anxiety about her future and always lived for today. Dottie was not always happy-go-lucky and compliant. She was feisty. Dancing with her sometimes became the Cha-Cha! If she wanted something or did not want to do something, there was not a thing that anyone could do except to wait and approach in a different way, choosing battles carefully. I would ask myself, how important is this? With Dottie I learned to use very few words and planned for her objections. I learned to not ask her to go somewhere or to do something. Instead I would just begin walking in the direction that I needed to go while holding her hand and demonstrating what I wanted her to do. If she asked me where we were going I would respond with "You'll see. It will be fun." or "Somewhere you will like." This worked about 85 percent of the time. The other 15 percent of the time I had no choice but to change my agenda. Moment by moment, Dottie and I walked together in the now! The gift of living in the moment is yet another life-changing lesson. Dottie taught me how to be present and enjoy each moment.

Living in the moment does not mean that you have to deny or ignore your past. On the contrary, acknowledging and accepting where we came from helps us learn to live in the moment. As we embrace who we are and where we have been, along with our lifetime of experiences, we become less fearful and free to be fully present today. Sometimes the past may not be pleasant but that does not diminish its significance. Everyone has a history.

Living in the moment does not mean that you are to have no concerns or plans for your future. It does mean that your future does not control your today. Yes, there are things and situations that require your attention. Planning is essential and is the wise person's path. Do not allow planning for the future to rob you of your joy today. Yes, you need to look ahead and plan, but do it with the right attitude. Do it consciously and deliberately without allowing it to steal and destroy this moment. Then you can lay the worries, concerns and regrets aside and be present. This lesson is for everyone, not just for caregivers. Everyone has the opportunity and ability to embrace and enjoy the present. It begins by clearing your mind of as many thoughts as possible.

Learning to clear your mind and just be present takes practice. Start by paying special attention to your environment. Notice the color of the sky and the sounds of the breeze. Stopping to smell the roses is a clear act of living in the now. So, literally, stop and smell the roses; touch the soft petals of the rose and feel the wonder of its beauty. While you are sitting or walking, just be. Look around and observe. Be fully present. This can be done for just a few minutes at a time until you get the hang of it. Once you feel the benefits of being fully present, you will want to make it a habit. It can help with stress and boost your immune system. Living in the moment and being fully present is a gift you can give yourself. As you gift yourself your calmness, empathy and presence begins to show. Your loved one living with dementia will begin responding positively, and your time together will become more enjoyable. Your time together begins to transform because you are learning to "Be." Enjoy!

It's not so difficult to practice living in the moment. Breathing and focusing on each breath is one way to start. Next, simply pay attention to what is happening right now, exactly where you are. If you are reading this book, do just that. Read this book, allowing yourself to become engrossed in the pages and fully enjoy the words. When you visit your loved one, pay attention to them as you listen to them and observe their actions. Engage them in conversation, empathize, smile, laugh and cry with them. Enjoy the process! Be! Focus on where they are and what is going on in their world. Just be present. There, in the moment, is another great gift you can give to your loved one with dementia -- your presence! Get out of your own thoughts and focus on the now. Just Be! Just be where you are with a total awareness of now.

As you practice living in the now, do not try too hard. If you try too hard, you may end up thinking about succeeding, thinking about what to do and what not to do, thinking about how hard you are trying to do it right. All this thinking may actually cause you to lose the present moment you wish to attain. It sounds crazy, but it is true. Simply relax, breathe and "Be." You may say to yourself, "I am here now and I am going to be fully present." Try to relax and enjoy without expectations. Just Be.

If you are a caregiver for someone with dementia, you probably put great expectations on yourself. You also have spent a great deal of time doing things for your loved one. Today, practice living in the moment.

The benefits of living in the moment cannot be overstated. You must step back and focus only on the present moment. Notice your environment. Notice what is good right where you are sitting or standing, smell the smells, see the sights, hear the music and look for the blessings. They are there, even in the worst of storms. There is always a rainbow. Sometimes it is hidden beneath the clouds of your circumstances, but it is always there. By living in the moment and experiencing the now, you will have the ability to see beyond circumstances and embrace today, one day at a time. You can learn to be fully present in the moment. Letting go of the past and the future, you will begin to truly live in the moment. Today is yours! Enjoy it, courtesy of the gift of living in the moment!

CHAPTER 7

The Walk Through Grief

"Sorrow prepares you for joy. It violently sweeps everything out of your house, so that new joy can find space to enter. It shakes the yellow leaves from the bough of your heart, so that fresh green leaves can grow in their place. It pulls up the rotten roots, so that new roots hidden beneath have room to grow. Whatever sorrow shakes from your heart, far better things will take their place."

— Jelaluddin Rumi, thirteenth century

Ralph is always pleasant. He has an inappropriate laughter response to most conversations, so one cannot help but smile when talking to him. Ralph's daughter, Mary, has not seen her father in 7 years. She was extremely disappointed in her father's careless attitude and lack of concern for his future. As Ralph's dementia progressed, he had made terrible financial decisions and refused to allow Mary to assist him. Without understanding that poor judgment and lack of reasoning often accompany dementia, Mary holds Ralph's poor choices against him and she is angry. Anger, itself, is not the issue. Rather, it is how the anger related to unresolved grief may distort and damage relationships. Mary laments, "If only he had listened to me. If only he would have moved in with me and allowed me to care for him."

Mary is Ralph's only child, and because of his mistakes she has removed herself from being part of Ralph's life. Mary has no contact with Ralph and refuses to visit. It is sad. I hear a concern and love for Ralph in his daughter's voice, but Mary is unable to let go of dreams and expectations she had for her father's life. His daughter had planned for Ralph's life to be different. Mary foresaw Ralph moving in with her in her elder years. Dementia was not in the plan.

This was not the way that things were supposed to work out. Mary is grieving.

It is certainly not what Ralph had planned either. He now has no family with whom to share his life. Everyone who meets Ralph adores him. Although he does have a few very dedicated caregivers, Ralph appears to silently long for his daughter. He gets particularly sad and quiet during holidays and family activities. The caregivers tend to go above and beyond their usual job description for Ralph's benefit. They sense his sadness and try to compensate by engaging him in their own family's life—even taking him home for holidays and special occasions. Ralph always responds to their kindness with a sweet yet empty smile. In his eyes something is lacking. Being a kind man, Ralph would never want anyone to think he did not appreciate his or her efforts. Trying to hide his grief, Ralph masks it with his smile and inappropriate laughter.

His daughter Mary's grief hides even deeper, disguised by anger, bitterness and denial. Mary is a daughter who honestly loves her father. The magnitude and denial of her grief immerses Mary in a downward spiral. Grief needs to be felt. Just like a volcano without a pressure release, it will escape. It may not release in an explosion, but it may trickle out, one life-poisoning attitude at a time. There is no way around it. You must walk through the grief if you want to see the gift that is still there for you and your loved one, even in the midst of grieving. Mary may have shut down her feelings. She, perhaps, is not willing, at this point, to acknowledge them. Possibly, her feelings are too painful or frightening, and Mary may be missing the opportunity to enjoy her father's companionship and love. Hopefully the day will come when Mary is ready to face her deep sorrow. The tools are available for her but it is a choice that she will have to make herself. You do not have to follow Mary's path. You can deal with your feelings of grief today.

Grief is a multifaceted response to loss. It can be devastating. When a loved one has dementia, some amount of grief is inevitable. The losses are immense - lost dreams and hopes can be overwhelming. Suddenly, nothing about your future makes sense. Everything is different. And tomorrow brings yet more grief. For the person living with dementia, both physical and emotional declines occur over a prolonged period. These changes can be emotionally and financially draining for the caregiver or family member.

Spouses and children of those with dementia often say they experience grief on a regular basis. Each interaction brings it to the forefront, again and again, sometimes on a daily basis. Is it possible, with all this grief, to live your life well, and to support and enjoy the person living with dementia? Yes it is possible, but not without first allowing yourself to fully experience your grief.

Dementia and Alzheimer's disease is very sad. You need to walk through the grief honestly. Dodging the grief can have many negative consequences. Avoidance can take on several forms including depression, anger and bitterness, working too much, substance abuse, isolating and minimizing feelings. To really feel the grief is a difficult path but completely necessary to live your best life possible. This process will take time and sincere effort, so be gentle with yourself as you acknowledge and walk through your grief, step by step.

With great tenderness, feel those feelings; anger, sadness, helplessness, despair. It's not only okay; it is necessary for your healing. Find an appropriate outlet for your emotions. Many people journal, which means setting aside time to write down everything they wish they could say to the person now living with dementia. Free write and say what you feel. You may feel disappointed and angry and find yourself writing "How could you do this to me?" There are no right or wrong words. Just write.

Another way to get those feelings out is to cry, laugh, scream, or punch a pillow. Just get them out. There are no rules. Find a quiet place where you can be alone, or invite a friend along for support. It is necessary to get those feelings out. In the case of dementia and ongoing grief, you definitely need to express your personal disappointments and sadness. Some people use sports and athletic activity. Working out in a gym or taking a brisk walk can elevate your mood and release the endorphins that naturally help ease pain, the "feel good" hormones. Physical activity provides that extra bonus.

Next, force yourself to be active in something that is important to you. Commit to not isolating yourself. Make a list of things that you used to enjoy and do at least one of those things weekly. Whether it is reading a book, walking through the mall or visiting the beach, just make sure you do something that you enjoy. Finding the time can be difficult, so try to find some help to care for the person with dementia. On some occasions you can take your loved one with you. Allow yourself to enjoy life. Prioritize time for yourself to do things that bring you peace and joy.

Simply relaxing and being with your feelings can have its place in your grief walk. Being alone with your pain is not a bad thing. Some days you may not feel like interacting. With no right or wrong ways to walk through this, the importance lies in pushing forward, despite your circumstances. It is extremely personal. Be cautious though, as too much alone time can be detrimental. Balance is key. Keep balance and perspective in check and allow yourself time to be sad. If things become too difficult, it is good to seek professional help. It may be necessary to help you over the big hurdles that stand in your way.

As you walk through grief, it is important to take time to be grateful. Each day, write a gratitude list, naming the really good things in your life. Thank your God for providing you with these things and for the time that you have had with your loved one living with dementia. He or she really is a gift to you. Being grateful helps immensely.

Finally, and extremely important, develop a personal support system. This is the single most powerful tool in your toolbox. There are groups nationwide that are available to provide information, education and connect you with others going through similar circumstances. This is a journey that you need not take alone; look for others willing to offer support and understanding. Family, friends and support groups are there for you. Multiple online resources are available. Seek them out. You will be glad you did. (See Resources at the end of this book.) Accepting and dealing with your grief is a wonderful gift for you to give to your loved one and to yourself.

Once you have dealt with your grief, you will be able to open up your heart to experience the joy that is still there when you interact with your loved one who has dementia. That person is still there. Many love-filled moments are yet to be shared. Once you have recognized and dealt with your own grief, perhaps you can help them to release some of theirs. Don't be afraid to follow their lead. Cry with them, scream with them and share these real emotions together. In a very special way, this can show your loved one that you are there for them, no matter what the future brings. See them as a whole person, not as their disease. As your heart heals, so can theirs. Be gentle with them and be gentle with yourself. Walking through your grief and theirs, with compassion and kindness, is the most tender of the gifts. It is a sacred process. Indeed, this is a very precious gift that you can give yourself and your loved one.

There is not enough that can be said about the benefits of living in the moment. To do this you must step back and look only at the present moment. Notice your environment. See the good, smell the smells and look for the blessings. They are there, even in the worst of storms. There is always a rainbow. Sometimes it is hidden beneath your clouds of circumstances, but it is always there. By living in the moment and experiencing the now, you will have the ability to see beyond circumstances and embrace today, one day at a time. You can learn to be fully present in the moment. Letting go of the past and not focusing on the future will allow you to truly live in the moment. Today is yours! Enjoy it, courtesy of the gift of living in the moment!

CHAPTER 8

The Great Need For Knowledge And Support

"Knowledge is power. Information is liberating.
Education is the premise of progress, in
every society, in every family."

- Kofi Annan

Margaret was obviously a classy lady. She had grown up in a financially well-to-do family and always enjoyed the finer things in life. After her husband's passing, Margaret's poor judgment surfaced. At first, her family attributed it to grief, but as her odd behaviors and poor hygiene increased, the family sensed that she was no longer making good decisions. During a visit Margaret's daughter, Sally, found a bank statement listing a cleared check for $11,000. She asked, "Mom, what is this?"

"None of your business," Margaret snapped.

Sally, not yet recognizing her mother's dementia, fought back the tears as her mother grabbed the bank statement and stormed out of the room. Sally initiated a family phone conference with her siblings, two brothers and one sister, who were not in agreement. The general consensus was that Margaret was fine and Sally needed to stay out of Mom's business. As months passed, Sally questioned her own judgment. Secretly, she began to investigate her mother's financial documents. What she found was shocking. Margaret had sent more than $70,000 to bank accounts around the world, from Jamaica to India; multiple transactions had taken place within the last six months. Sally called another conference with her family. This time, they paid attention and decided to confront their mother. As you can imagine, that meeting did not go well.

Margaret denied transferring funds and became irate and defensive. Suspecting exploitation, her family notified the sheriff's department and asked Margaret to allow an investigation. Margaret finally showed them a drawer full of international lottery forms. She told them that she had won $5,000,000 and sent the payments to cover processing fees and international taxes. Because all the money was sent out of the United States, there was little that could be done. The sheriff's department told Margaret that these were not legitimate lotteries and that her money was being stolen. Margaret argued and could not be convinced that these people had lied. She continued to send them money despite all the warnings. The more the family tried to intervene, the more determined Margaret was to hide her international deposits. She claimed that these people were her friends. She was certain that she had won this money, and she accused her children of being jealous and wanting to deprive her of her winnings. Margaret took her wedding rings and heirloom jewelry to a pawnshop and sold them for cash to send additional funds to her "friends."

Her family watched as Margaret squandered more than $350,000. Attempts to reason with Margaret failed, and she alienated herself from her children. Sally was distraught and powerless. What would become of her mother? How would she survive? Unfortunately, no advanced planning had taken place and Margaret was considered legally competent to make these decisions. Sally stood alone in her attempts to help her mother. Although her siblings now believed her, Sally was left to deal with the situation without any assistance from them. They were uncertain regarding their mother's dementia and did not want to further strain their relationships with their mother. Not knowing what to do, Sally pressed on alone until she found a local support group. She found solace there and began to learn everything that she could about dementia. This helped her to explore her options and enabled her to pave a path to help her mother. Knowledge is power.

Eventually Margaret had a complete medical and mental examination and was diagnosed with dementia. Their mother-daughter relationship had nearly crumbled, and Sally relied heavily on the support network she had developed. This was tough love; doing the right thing for her mother despite the extreme emotional difficulty and alienation. The lesson here is to listen to your gut and seek support and assistance early. This gift is found in knowledge and support. There are many books, websites, local and regional resources available to help you increase your personal knowledge of dementia. Don't wait until circumstances have spun out of control. Plan ahead and stay informed.

All of us need advanced planning to be prepared. Elder law attorneys can assist you with developing a road map including financial and future health care decisions while you are still able to make decisions. They will help you navigate successfully on this journey before issues arise. Use your insight and prepare yourself. A multitude of problems can arise if you wait too long to seek assistance. In addition to local resources, there are several national organizations promoting education about dementia and Alzheimer's awareness, such as the Alzheimer's Association, www.alz.org.

(See list of resources at the end of this book.) Be resourceful and seek wisdom, remembering that you are capable. Your unique inner guidance can nag away at your soul when things are not quite right. You may have experienced that faint voice and tried to ignore it. Know that it is not your imagination. Become educated, listen and act accordingly, but most importantly, take time to listen to your inner voice. When you sense that something is going on, seek guidance from people who have experience and knowledge. They are available to help you every step along the way.

Eventually, Sally was able to protect her mother's remaining assets and secure Margaret's financial future. Seeking guidance early can often change your path and lessen the overwhelming state of affairs that can develop. Perhaps, if Sally had listened to herself when she first saw the signs and felt that something was wrong, the losses and related stress could have been prevented.

The importance of preplanning cannot be stressed enough. Even early in dementia, one may begin to lose the ability to think logically. Because of the lack of judgment and their ability to disguise their memory issues, people with dementia are often taken advantage of and exploited by strangers, friends, acquaintances and even family members. Preplanning and seeking assistance early is key. If no plan exists, it is extremely important to be aware of your loved one's financial and personal activities. If something does not seem quite right, it probably is not. Follow your instincts, ask questions and seek guidance. Put into place a plan for the future, including advanced directives and a power of attorney. With or without such a plan, family members and close friends need to learn how to recognize the signs of dementia. Sally, Margaret's daughter, knew that things were not quite right but did not follow her instincts, initially. She doubted herself until circumstances escalated. Exploring options, before a crisis occurs, is exercising your God-given wisdom. Trust your own inner alarm. If possible, prepare for any circumstances that you or a loved one may face. Seek guidance and support. At any age, regardless of your health status, preplanning is wise.

Knowledge and support are vital. You will need other people to hold you up, if you are to survive this journey through dementia. It is not a journey that you should walk through alone. Others have been down this road and have practical tips, wisdom, strength and hope to share. They are able to listen and truly hear what you are saying. Being heard will give you strength. Sometimes, just feeling validated can make all the difference in the world. You are not alone.

It is essential for you to locate support groups and people with whom you can connect comfortably. Open yourself up to try different groups until you find the one(s) that feel right for you. Some people find they benefit more from one-on-one counseling sessions. Regardless of how and where you discover support services, find your best fit and take advantage of this enormous gift. Do not opt out, as this gift, too, can be life-changing. There are also many online support services and blogs available. The important thing is to find the fit that feels right for you. Seek out a group or individual that feels safe and enables you to listen, relate and be heard. Many local and national resources are available and can be discovered through connecting with others. Reach out and pursue knowledge and information. Know that this journey is much better with a village of support.

Open yourself up to receive and you will be amazed at what is available. Honestly, you are not alone. This gift of support is the lifeboat of your journey. Choose to grab hold of it and live with knowledge, strength and confidence again.

CHAPTER 9

Climbing the Mountain to Eternity

**"It is never a tragedy when an old man, who
has lived a good life, passes away."**

**Spoken to me at my father's death; a rephrasing of a
quote from Prairie Home Companion by Garrison Keillor**

During the hospice visit that day, the nurse told us that dad would be with us for at least another week. My sister and I did not agree, but we thought that perhaps we were too close to the situation to be able to evaluate it. We doubted our assessment and instinct, but sensed something was changing. My nephew, who was also my dad's first grandson and my sister's first born child, was flying out to Afghanistan in just a few hours. He had scheduled with us to call that evening before boarding his plane. My sister and I knew that this would probably be the last time that Dad and his grandson would talk, as communication would be very limited during his deployment to Afghanistan.

Dad seemed to be losing his strength, rapidly. His eyes remained closed most of the time; his words had become difficult to understand.

To clear our heads and prepare for the evening, my sister and I took a walk through a nearby state park. A magnificent hawk made a special appearance that day. We felt this was an awesome gift, knowing that Dad, having been a great lover of the outdoors, would have delighted in seeing the hawk and in the symbolism of its appearance. The beautiful hawk sought us out and called to us, three times, as if to say, "Time to go home!" It left a great peace in our hearts, as we felt the hawk was sending a message that Dad's time had come. We followed our instincts and headed back to our father.

Arriving at our dad's home, we found out that my nephew had just called and said his goodbyes. Dad had awakened and tried very hard to speak to his grandson, muttering a few words. He had not opened his eyes since the phone call about 6:00 pm. The next two hours were the final hours of Dad's life.

We began our bedside vigils so Dad was not alone for a moment. Despite the nurse's evaluation, we followed our own instincts. We knew that something was changing; we sensed a transition. As he lay motionless, my sister and I sat on one side of the bed, and my stepmother sat on the other side. I was holding his hand and my sister had placed her hand on Dad's heart.

Several weeks earlier, I was privileged to have had a meaningful conversation with my dad: "Dad, you had told me many years ago, that when your time came, you wanted to walk into the woods, climb the mountain and sit at the foot of a tree. Dad, when your time comes, I will hold your hand as you climb the mountain."

Dad smiled and we talked about the mountains. I told him that my sister would be there too. He looked directly in my eyes and said, "That's good to know Wendy. I needed to know that." I sensed his understanding and let it go.

Now, here we were, just as we had discussed in that conversation weeks ago. Dad's time had come for his journey up the mountain. We knew that his destiny was calling; the tremendous agony of losing our father groaned inside our hearts. We had no idea how to be there for him or how to be there for each other. It was extremely difficult to follow our instincts and just be.

Here we were, gathered around his hospital bed, trying to be present for him in the midst of our overwhelming grief. We had known that this day was coming and had thought that we were prepared, but now, everything that we thought we knew, no longer made sense. The thought of losing him forever was unbearable, yet here we were. His time had come. We had to ultimately "be" in the moment. Our dad was dying and we had no idea what to do.

My sister took the lead as we began to walk with him up the mountain. As she started to bring the visualization of the walk through the woods, my dad's breathing pattern changed. She guided him to the edge of the woods. His breaths became rapid and deep, as if he were running. We held tight and described the mountainside. "Let's go up the mountain Dad." Gently describing the scene, smells and feelings of the outdoors, he began to respond. "We are here Dad, it's all up to you now. We love you so much and we are here. Run Dad, run up the mountain." Dad's breathing increased, as he showed us a glimpse into his spiritual journey. My sister and I encouraged him. And he made the climb, with us by his side.

I honestly can't tell you how long he traversed as time stood still. We had traveled into a spiritual vortex, of sorts, as we joined in his determination to reach the top. I remember my sister almost shouting, saying, "You go Dad! You're like a gazelle, leaping up that mountain." "You're like a deer, springing through the woods." "Go Dad," we echoed. Then he arrived. With a slight exhale. Dad had arrived. It was beautiful, yes, beautiful. My sister jumped up and opened the bedroom window and cheered his spirit onto his next life. We were ecstatic. We hugged him, laughed and cried, all at the same time. He had reached the mountaintop.

This was the single most significant event of my life and God's greatest gift to me. I was both humbled and elated. My sister and I had just escorted my father to the other side. I had not known this was possible. Any doubt of his destiny was instantly removed, and my sadness was overshadowed by the miraculous journey I had just witnessed. It was such an incredible experience. My dad had climbed his mountain to eternity and I had the honor of participating. During his death, I had never felt more alive, having stood in the gap between life and death, and I sensed it was that way for him, too. My sister and I were there and were able to be completely present for the moment. Thank you, Dad.

Death is not always this beautiful, but it is always significant. When your loved one begins to prepare for passing, you may not be ready. You can try to prepare yourself in advance and if possible, prepare your loved one, too. Talk about it when the opportunity presents itself. Don't allow your fear and grief to stand in the way of authentic communication. As you work through this, you will discover that fear and grief are very real and significant parts of it all. Through my dad's transition, I experienced a full range of emotions. I felt the feelings, but did not allow them to prohibit me from being present. You, too, can be present, despite your emotions. Allow your feelings to be felt.

You can begin your preparation by facing your own fear of death. It may help to read chapter two again. As you become comfortable with your own mortality, you will be better able to let go and "Be." This is not an easy journey but is very worth the effort.

The irony is that while preparation helps you to have some awareness, everything that you think you know and everything that you have prepared for may simply dissolve into the moment. That is perfectly fine. Be willing to go with the flow. Death is as much a part of life as birth is. It is a rebirth of sorts into a new life, and we never lose our loved ones in our hearts. It is there that we keep them alive in spirit. With Alzheimer's and dementia, the final stages can be extremely heartbreaking. Many of you will feel like your loved one dies long before the physical body ceases to exist. You are not alone. This time of their life can be unsettling and grievous. Call on your support people and ask for what you need. As body functions begin to fail, your loved one may become less and less responsive to your presence. This may linger for days, weeks and even months. Please know that, even at this stage, they hear your voice and can sense your presence. Believe it or not, this, too, is a gift.

As you wait for death to take the physical body, the opportunity for spiritual healing abounds. It can be a bittersweet space; a time when emotions are vivid and fluctuating. Try not to judge yourself. Allow yourself to be present and call on your best support people. During these days, weeks or months, know that your loved one is still the person you love. That person is still here. Talk, sing, laugh, play music and reminisce with your loved one. Share how their life influenced you and why you are a better person because of them. Offer touch and presence. If there remain any matters that are not yet resolved, take this opportunity to resolve them. As one waits, guilt and regrets may surface for both of you. The person dying may have issues that are unresolved and unsettling. You may wish that things had been better in your relationship. Now is the time to let go and usher in forgiveness.

Let them know that you forgive them, ask for forgiveness and talk them through forgiving themselves. Your loved one can hear you. This is your chance to put the past behind and set your loved one free. Speak prayers of peace and healing. I once prayed with a woman who was very close to death. As I prayed for peace and healing, I could sense her spirit receiving total healing and total peace as she released her body to death. It was complete. No more pain or disease.

Sometimes there will be family members who cannot participate. For whatever reason, they cannot offer forgiveness or cannot let go. Just know that everyone copes with death in his or her own unique way. This, too, is okay. You can act as a surrogate and offer healing words regarding the situation or absence of a significant family member. It may be as simple as "Dad, you know that Denise loves you. She will be okay. Look how strong she is. We know that she will be okay. She just has to work some things out... Look how well she has done in her career. That is from your influence. You taught us the value of hard work..." You get the approach. You can stand in for someone unwilling or unable to resolve issues. This can bring great peace to someone on the threshold of departure.

When peace and forgiveness have manifested, the process becomes more natural and gentle. Although not without tears and distress, the struggle often appears to lessen as pure love fills the room. Both you and the dying person will sense this. Once you are liberated from the guilt and fear, you are able to be present in a sincere and honest way. You will be able to leave the bedside and know that if they pass while you are absent, things are unfolding exactly as they are meant to. The final gift is the greatest gift of all. It is love, pure and true love. This, too, is part of your journey through dementia and it is yours forever. You can know, beyond any doubt, that he or she is passing into eternal peace. You have held hands through the journey, honoring your loved one and the life you shared. Open the window and set your loved one free.

CHAPTER 10

Where Do We Go
From Here?

"God put the rainbow in the clouds, not just in
the sky ... It is wise to realize we already have
rainbows in our clouds, or we wouldn't be here.
If the rainbow is in the clouds, then in the worst
of times, there is the possibility of seeing hope ...
We can say, 'I can be a rainbow in the cloud for
someone yet to be.' That may be our calling."

Maya Angelou, Harrisburg Forum (30 November 2001)

Dementia and Alzheimer's disease will bring a storm into your life. There is no doubt about that. But be assured that there is always a rainbow to be found. Look for it. It may be found in your reconnecting with a person going through this disease. It may be revealed in a way that you never could have imagined. You may discover things you never knew about your loved one. And the things that you learn about yourself may be life changing. With lessons to be learned and, yes, memories to be shared and enjoyed, I encourage you to find the rainbow. It is not far above the clouds. Open your gifts today and begin this difficult, yet incredible journey.

The first gift is learning to communicate beyond words. My dad taught me this in a deep and meaningful way. I so appreciate him and his lesson. Sometimes talking is good. There are things that need to be said. Other times, being present and silent can reveal the true picture of who you actually are. This in turn, can open great doors of natural, sincere connection. Sincere connection takes place as we relax into our own authentic self. Learn to just "be." That is enough. That is love. The person living with dementia can sense your true being without words. It is the gift of honest, heartfelt communication.

The second gift, dealing with your fears, may quite possibly be your breakthrough gift. As you take this step, things will begin to shift. Dementia is packed with fear, an extremely heavy bag to carry. Everyday, fear fights for center stage of your life and can affect every area of your life. It weakens your immune system, interferes with sleep, causes heartache and destroys lives. Once you acknowledge its stronghold and choose to face it head on, healing begins. Elizabeth received a healing by facing her fears. She was both courageous and beautiful, so are you. Look at all you have already survived. You are not a stranger to challenges. Face your fears and live in strength.

The third gift is learning that you can make a difference in the lives of people living with dementia. You have the power inside you to get through this, one step at a time. This can seem like a daunting responsibility, and it is. But it is not more than you can manage. Today, this is where you are, and you do have choices. Choices that can and will change lives, yours included. This gift is very powerful. Joe's family knew how to approach and accept Joe, the quiet gentle man, in a way that allowed him to live with dementia. His caregivers wanted to do the right thing, but they lacked the experience and know how. Once they were taught, Joe thrived. You do make a huge difference.

The fourth gift is letting go, and can be the most costly gift. It is the ultimate gift you can give to your loved one. The epitome of love is demonstrated in the act of allowing your loved one to be who they are right now and loving them exactly where they are. They need you now more then ever, and it is a time when your emotional strength will be challenged. Paul, the loving husband, eventually was able to let go. It was not without a fight, but he did survive. He is now able to speak to others about his journey from a very deep and personal place. He is an amazing, good, kind man.

The fifth gift, recognizing and appreciating your marvelous mind, helps you to change your perspective. It opens doors of possibilities. Patricia, living well in her own reality, demonstrates that your perception changes everything. When you allow yourself to see things from a different angle, things look different. Look and see the wonderful lesson that she teaches. Your own magnificent mind can learn to perceive things differently. Regardless of the circumstances, you can change your focus and perception to really see the good things around you. The greater the attention on the positives, the larger they become. Conversely, if you focus on the negative, that will increase. Where you focus your mind truly affects your reality. Learn to see the rainbow in the clouds, even during the worst of storms.

The sixth gift is about learning how to be right where you are and be completely okay about it. Dottie, the feisty Italian, demonstrates this so well. She lives for today. The gift of living in the moment changes lives by changing your attention. Concentrating on right where you are at any given moment is key to being present. Looking at each moment alone can free up space in your life to really experience joy. This can also be extremely enlightening. As you experience your immediate environment and scenario, life happens. It is associated with stopping to smell the roses and enjoying the act of now. Notice the endless possibilities as you begin to walk in joy next to your person with dementia, right now. Today is really what matters in their reality. You can become part of that, by following their lead and by not trying to pull them into your world, instead walk in theirs, beside them in the now.

Gift number seven; dealing with grief is the sacred gift. Walking through grief can be heart wrenching. Ralph and Mary, the estranged father and daughter, may never be reconciled. This is extremely sad for both of them. As you grieve and heal, there is a rebirth of sorts that takes place. New life sprouts up where grief once lived. As difficult as it can be to walk through grief, this gift is life giving. It does not mean that you will not be sad. Quite the opposite actually occurs. Sad feelings are real feelings. The more you attempt to squash them, the stronger they tend to become. Instead of squashing them, let them be felt. Allow them to come out in a safe way with the support people that you grow to trust. In doing so, you make room for the joy and the laughter yet to be shared.

This is embraced in the eighth gift of knowledge, strength and support. The rainbow may be seen in the eyes of the people that rise up to assist you during this storm. Many of them may become lifelong friends. The deep understanding that you may find will be there forever. Knowledge, strength and support embody the lifeboats that can save your life. Sally, the daughter who was alone in her journey, survived because of the support she found.

Lastly, the greatest gift is the gift of love. This gift from God is the final gift. It lives forever in your life. Because of this journey you are different, in a good way. Perhaps you are more patient, more tolerant or more giving. You may have discovered things about yourself that you never imagined; your strength, your stamina and your creativity.

Your journey is difficult, but there is a rainbow. There remains always, some light through the storm. In the midst of it, you may become weather beaten and are often unable to look up. That is perfectly understandable.

Please be with your pain and disappointment when and how you need to be. Take time for you, exactly where you are. Try to reach out and find the people who are there for you when you can. Perhaps you will be the one to be there for someone who needs your experience to help get through a similar journey. Beyond our understanding, this is another hidden gift— a light in darkness and a rainbow in the storm.

The final days of this journey may show your brightest rainbow. Things that have been swept under the table for years may surface and present an opportunity for the greatest healing of your life. As you are presented an opportunity to lay it on the table and let it all go with love and forgiveness, step up boldly. It may be the most emotionally painful time of your life, yet the greatest healing. The irony of it all does not seem to make sense, but somehow it comes forth. While feeling loss and devastation, how can you possibly heal? You have also been living with this disease. In many ways, it can be harder on you than it is on the person with dementia. You may have had to be the strong one. You may have had to handle a large proportion of day-to-day decisions on your own. You may have had to make huge sacrifices daily to survive this disease. You are, also, in a very big way, living with dementia.

My experience has been that people with dementia have a beautiful inner place that is still able to experience your presence at all stages of the disease. When you are able to connect, and only after connecting, there is a place inside your loved one that you can sometimes reach. It is what I call the inner self. The inner self is not what we do or what we say. It is that part inside each of us that holds the center of who we are and is closely connected to your emotions. You have heard it is said that people will not remember what you said or what you did but they will remember how you made them feel. It appears that the same occurs with people with dementia by way of their inner self. It is not so much about your actions or your words, although they do set the stage, but it is more about how you make the person with dementia feel.

The people with dementia who came into my care did not know me prior to their diagnosis, yet they recognized me at every visit. It is not the memory of me that came forth. Rather it was their recognizing and recalling on some level, how I made them feel. Not remembering my name or understanding how they knew me, they perceived that I loved and enjoyed their presence and they recognized on a deeper level that I was there for them. This message, somehow, reached their soul. It crossed over into their inner self and a connection was made. You, too, can have this connection. It will be an everlasting gift for both of you, a gift experienced in the moment.

Your loved one with dementia is still with you. They are just different because their brain is failing, nothing more, nothing less. As you face this journey with them, they may not have comprehension as you and I do, but they get it. As you speak to their inner self, they get it. They may not be able to show you, but they get it. Just be, give and receive. At the same time, take care of yourself. Know that, if your loved one were able to choose, that is what he/she would choose for you.

Healing, love and forgiveness, it's all there. This disease affects the brain and the person is still there! That person is still your parent, grandparent, spouse or beloved friend. Things are just different now, and the person with dementia cannot change. The good news is, you can change. It is not an easy journey. In fact, this may be the most challenging time of your life. However, with personal education, preplanning when possible, introspection and a strong network of support, you can thrive while living with dementia and you can make a difference in the quality of life for your loved one and for yourself. You can choose to enjoy your journey together, in every moment possible. Instead of running and hiding from this storm, embrace it. I promise, it will make a difference in both of your lives. Reach for living your best life possible and offer that opportunity to your loved one by modeling that behavior. This endeavor will not be effortless, but you can find the rainbow. Know that your loved ones with this disease cannot change. It has to be you who looks up to search the clouds for the rainbow. Yes, this is a difficult journey, but you are not alone. Hold each other up, connect with support people and allow yourself to receive. At the same time, be innovative and discover your own solutions. You have everything that you need already inside you. Trust your instincts, be courageous and look up. See how far you have come and recognize your inner strength. You are amazing. You will see love in your rainbow if you look for it. It is the choosing to search that makes the difference. See it now in the midst of the storm. It is the greatest gift of all. Love. Receive it!

AUTHOR BIO

Wendy Wells-Chanampa is a Registered Professional Guardian with expertise in senior care, a Certified Dementia Care Practitioner and Certified Dementia Care Trainer through the National Council of Certified Dementia Practitioners and International Council of Certified Dementia Practitioners. She is also a Certified PAC (Positive Approach to Care) Dementia Care Trainer through Teepa Snow, MS, OTR/L, FAOTA.

Wendy is extremely passionate about dementia care, focused on enhancing the quality of life for those affected. She flows with compassion and integrity. With more than 30 years experience working with elders, she has extensive experience in dementia awareness.

Wendy studied health care administration at Penn State University and is a certified senior center manager. In 2008, she became a registered guardian and started Senior Resource Consultants, Inc. Her practice includes care management, family counseling and caregiver training, along with education about effectively interacting with people who have dementia and Alzheimer's disease. Her love of this population is evident in her training sessions and interactions.

Having spent a lifetime acquiring experience in the dementia care field, Wendy has developed her natural ability for relating to this population successfully. Her unique hands-on approach, real life stories and experiential learning are evident in her compelling story telling. She is a frequent keynote speaker at events and conferences focused on caring for Alzheimer and dementia patients. She is also the host of seminars for teaching effective coping mechanisms and care strategies to other caregivers and care organizations.

Resources for Information and Support

Help is a phone call away:

Alzheimer's Association 24/7 Helpline: 1-800-272-3900

Alzheimer's Foundation of America Helpline: 1-866-232-8484

Friendship Line (offered by the Institute on Aging) Hotline: 1-800-971-0016

Online Resources:

www.alzheimers.net

www.alz.org/we_can_help_24_7_helpline.asp

http://www.alzfdn.org

www.alzsupport.org

www.alzheimersreadingroom.com

www.burzynskilaw.com

www.lifeandmemorycenter.com

www.neuropsychstudies.com

www.lbda.org

www.lcplfa.org

www.nia.nih.gov/alzheimers

www.pasfi.org

www.parkinson.org

www.teepasnow.com